ODETTE

✻

ODETTE

❊

SARA
GELSTON

NEW MICHIGAN PRESS
TUCSON, ARIZONA

NEW MICHIGAN PRESS
DEPT OF ENGLISH, P. O. BOX 210067
UNIVERSITY OF ARIZONA
TUCSON, AZ 85721-0067

<http://newmichiganpress.com>

Orders and queries to <nmp@thediagram.com>.

Copyright © 2016 by Sara Gelston.
All rights reserved.

ISBN 978-1-934832-55-3. FIRST PRINTING.

Printed in the United States of America.

Design by Ander Monson.

Cover Art: Strauss Bourque-LaFrance, *Bonnet for the Best Shaker.*

CONTENTS

Odette   1

Acknowledgments   31

In the beginning there was talk of constant light,
annual tidal waves to clear out errors, a ban on all forms

of nostalgia. The new world was asking for wants
so I sent off my list: music with personal meaning,

pilgrimages for self's sake, some feelings ranked for translation.
To spoil the end, I wasn't given a window or door,

but a boat, blindfold. To spoil the beginning, I was given an oar.
Shown the way to skim water over the top like a breath.

≡

The radio tells me I'm in the world now, though I didn't ask for it.
Too bad, so sad was a thing some people would say.

I wanted to join in a movement so I snaked my body
through the streets, spoke out on some things and kept silent

on others. It seemed if I showed the right amount of life
I'd draw the right amount of attention. The radio tells me this

next song is called *Odette* and I think funny, that's also what
I'm called, though no one has called me that before,

though it's not funny,
though I wasn't here just yesterday.

≡

And if I say to you now *let's go*,
in which direction would you head?
It's romantic to imagine *west*
because histories, wagons, warmth.
It's useless to imagine *in*
because I can't join you. That's yours.
This is mine. To say *home* is to say
a recently invented name. The old one
was leveled, burned, cross-stitched
on some flag. It does no use to recall
what we once worked so hard to leave.

≡

Four times at the museum.
Four times I saw the same exhibit,
the Ellsworth Kelly print called
The River. Four times I was next
to someone who thought it looked
nothing like a river, that it looked
like a four year old had pulled
a black marker down a white page
over and over again. Four times
I thought this is what others
just imagine the world to be.
Four times I thought they don't remember.
I said it was meant to be the Seine,
the Rhine, though in their world the words
meant little. What are the rivers called now,
I wondered. What do the others want
a river to reflect. This one gave exactly
what I needed. Four times I stared for hours,
wrote down this river as a want.

≡

The radio tells me this weather is unnatural. The world too:
the men in it do unnatural things and the women work
to clear an unnaturally high bar. We don't remember
who hung it. It was only there when we arrived.
Each thing feels unpreventable. Too few people are excited
for this future, which is frightening, since who will hoist it?
Who will carry the buildings north on their backs? Who will dig
the holes? For me, because I can't see the end of this the future
is simply the oar cutting in. Its death also feels unpreventable,
but today the sky is calm. I found a rhythm and I'm going with it.
It's unreasonable to think each day is made for grace.

≡

If I've learned the new language right, lonely is now silent.

The pamphlet said it. The radio repeated. We must practice.

I've been feeling very silent these days.

I hung a silent sheet out the window to dry.

I've spent too many silent days thinking silent thoughts to myself.

I'm so silent, I say to the small mirror I was given.

The astronaut felt silent in space, the pamphlet gave as an example. We must practice.

The astronaut felt silent, so placed a flag in the ground to quiet it.

The woman was silent and met a silent man. Together, they're no longer silent, or are, but no longer say it.

We must say it.

The radio interrupts,
only the silent know the way I feel tonight.

Sometimes we should admit the translation is better.

Sometimes I'm sure the dial must be turned.

≡

Everything's the same just faster.
The speedboat speeds past the onlookers.
The women on board wave wild.
The music on shore clicks a frantic dance
and the shore girls twirl and dip and tire.
The night winds up and it winds down
and who is doing all this winding?
Who didn't write *something slow, please*
as a want? Who, I want to know,
is reading our desires?

≡

In all the paintings all the men
    know how to row. In all the paintings
women sit back as though a ghost
    force will deliver them to love or doom
because these are the only doors.
    Their bones are soft in their dresses.
They're rarely given oars.
    I give up.
Lady of Shalott will always die.
    Monet's pink ladies in their pink skiff
know the score. They're innocent
    because what else? They lean in
because no one should hear them ask
    is the coast clear?
Do you know which direction is out?

≡

I've been ending each day with a question:
Where is the moon? Can we edit this
new world how we need it? Can I find
a mode of transportation from where I am
to where you are? Science is awful and gives me awful dreams.
When will someone invent the machine
that captures the voice of the dead not in a box
but a room where they toast their glasses,
ask *does this make it easier?* I often toast but not too much.
I've been ending the night with the thought
I haven't forgotten you, though it's funny since I have.
It's been so long, it isn't funny anymore.
Our poor memories aren't funny and this place is a joke.
When will someone invent the button to go back?

≡

We've all been let go
from jobs we were good at.

I was good at sorting
what others needed

but kept forgetting
my shoes. I was good

at killing time back when
that was a trendy thing to do.

I killed cafes. Nights
with men. I am killing

this job of rowing
which is what scares me.

What next? What next?
I don't want to do the thing

I know they know
I was made for.

≡

In comes one man and in comes another
and of course they claim they know me
and of course I just say sure. It's simpler
most days to go with the flow so
I shut my mouth, float verily down the stream.
Yes, this is how I remember her, I hear both men say
from the shore. Sure, this is how you remember me,
I hear myself think then stop.

☰

To spoil the middle: the world
is a tough place to chew
your way through. No one famous
will say this. I sent up a handful
of letters with a handful of birds
and now a handful of people
believe I love them when I don't.
What's this curse that has me
confessing the right thing
to the wrong person? How now,
with only two remaining birds,
can I still not tell the one who
carries from the one who calls?

≡

The radio plays a familiar song. It sounds like the season
where everyone begins to imagine their lives

in warmer places, what might have been
if only this, if given that. I don't remember

the name of that season. I don't remember
the name for this feeling. There are times

I've been sure that everything is a game,
that we are awake and dry and living

in a Portuguese town. I've been told enough
times what isn't true. I'm sure I saw us

walking down a street, through a painting, in a home
someone claimed was burned. Who could pull off

such a hoax? This new world is strange,
but please tell me how strange.

≡

Our mock orange was lovely
back when the word was sincere.
This was before the mock wars,
mock talks, before the mock flag,
real weather, future feels. I don't want
magazines to tell me what's authentic anymore.
I want these mock messages to tell me
this new name is a mock mock joke.
If you keep asking, *who's there, who's there,*
I'll finally respond, *who is there?*
It's me, I guess I should say.
Remember me, little mocking me?

≡

Archipelago is a word
that means nothing now,
like freckle or fun times,
like the litany of Good Terms
they've chosen not to renew.

I'm writing a letter to the constable.

I'm writing a letter to you
to request visitation, skinny dips,
lake fucking at noon.

In *The Dictionary of Accepted Ideas*,
an empress is all beautiful
which I don't doubt was true.

When was the last time anyone saw a kingdom?

Where are the towers and the bugles?
Where are the queens? Is this water
I row the ocean or the world's largest moat?

≡

Out here, I've made muscles
I didn't know I had.

I wrote my name and yours
on a rock that said *we were here,*

the year, and drew a heart because it shows
we're in a place and we're in a time and we're trying.

Nature is a surface. I'm getting better
at skimming it. I found a place

that was a replica of a place I'd loved
only everyone had left. It was just like the episode

of that show everyone would talk about
but now no one remembers. All these years

I imagined a surprise looked one way
when of course it looked another.

≡

This situation faces two ways: It's a chance. It's a punishment.

I was part of a movement that marched with atrocities
printed on large posters. We were told the new world
must to be visual. I recorded on my poster the list

of places that no longer existed but everyone had
their own list, their own poster which told anyone passing
this happened to me or *I lived there* or *I have desires, please help.*

All of those people I marched with have been marched out, too.
They were given their own mode of transport and told
don't get off, don't get off, you're filled with grief, it's spreading.

≡

Has this new flood
reached you? Am I

reaching you now
underwater? Here,

half a street opened
up and a pit bull

guards the break.
I'm alone here

and eyeing a new silent
place to be. Are you

boiling your water
as we're told to? Are you

writing your aubades?
I keep thinking the sun

is coming but then it doesn't
and I go about my day.

Please send some new word
regarding the progress of the raft.

☰

1) Envision your life as a raft.
2) Come close to touching someone else, then withdraw.
3) Wake early and predict—calm day, or storm day?
4) Recall the feeling of grief. Feel grief.
5) Put your hand in water. Feel grief.

≡

When everything began to be bad for you
I quit everything. Red meat. Staring at Jupiter.
Stealing paintings. Inhaling alone. It was difficult
to escape the fear so I decided to swim.
My mistake. I didn't know then how far
the fear of others might take me. What could go
wrong with asking why this fear at this hour?
Why not the real fear I see forming overhead?

≡

In all the paintings I keep losing
    myself in the minutiae.
The Dutch bowl of berries
    or the blurred horse toward the back.
The signature folded at the edge of the scene.
    I'm killing time. I'd like to
step into the action but someone's always locking the door.
    I'd like to find a spot not next to
the muskets or dogs, the large ships
    or federal halls. I was told to be a vision
and I've been trying. I was told to be an image
    but I have issues staying still.
My boat is filling. I'm bailing.
    I keep going back to those berries,
the smallest one at the edge,
    that little one threatening to go.

≡

It's too difficult to know all the myths
so I've stopped trying. You're a myth
and so am I. Heat rises. Water too.
Hearts rise in water. Bodies sink
when weighted down by cinder blocks,
suitcases of dirt, late model trucks.
There's logic and then there's now.
Remember when the morning alarm would sound?
A myth: that we had some place to be.
A bigger myth: stay where you are
if you want someone to find you.
I'm moving on. You still know
which direction I'll head.

≡

Praise someone, I saw a light
in the distance and I thought
praise the painting with the light
that hung on the wall in our old
light-drowned life. Praise lonely light,
I miss the ease of standing
in a doorway seeing you from behind.
Now, I'm constantly wet. I can't sleep.
I'd like to forget about that painting
but I keep imaging it floating down
some river, two otters using it as a home,
tossing each other off one end
only to rescue each other from the other,
which is a kind of comfort, I'll admit,
praise someone, this long tonight.

≡

Slowly, the future is revealing
itself and slowly I forget which route
I took to get here. The radio plays the old songs
in a new way, which few people like, but agree
is better than silence. Those things we missed
we still miss, but the miss is now called remember.
I remember you, I'm told to practice, although I don't.
I remember you, you hated swimming, and the sense
of not touching the ground. In *The Dictionary
of Accepted Ideas*, the moon induces melancholy
and may be inhabited. Is that where they sent you,
paddling through the dark? It's springtime here,
or so I'm told. They say it could rain tomorrow.

ACKNOWLEDGMENTS

This chapbook makes several references to Gustave Flaubert's *The Dictionary of Accepted Ideas*, published in 1954.

Several of these sections appeared in *DIAGRAM*.

SARA GELSTON is the recipient of a 2015 Creative Writing Fellowship from the National Endowment for the Arts, and has been awarded fellowships and awards from the Fine Arts Work Center in Provincetown, the Wisconsin Institute for Creative Writing, and the University of Illinois, where she received her MFA. Her recent work appears in *Ploughshares, Best New Poets, Poetry Northwest,* and elsewhere. Originally from Maine, she lives in Indianapolis.

❁

COLOPHON

Text is set in a digital version of Jenson, designed by Robert Slimbach in 1996, and based on the work of punchcutter, printer, and publisher Nicolas Jenson. The titles here are in Futura.

❋

NEW MICHIGAN PRESS, based in Tucson, Arizona, prints poetry and prose chapbooks, especially work that transcends traditional genre. Together with DIAGRAM, NMP sponsors a yearly chapbook competition.

DIAGRAM, a journal of text, art, and schematic, is published bimonthly at THEDIAGRAM.COM. Periodic print anthologies are available from the New Michigan Press at NEWMICHIGANPRESS.COM.

www.ingramcontent.com/pod-product-compliance
Lightning Source LLC
Chambersburg PA
CBHW031507040426
42444CB00007B/1234